MW01148162

Brandi Dise

Under My Skin: Bones and Moonlight

Wider Perspectives Publishing ¤ 2023 ¤ Hampton Roads, Va.

© 2023, Brandi Dise,
1st run complete in November 2023
Wider Perspectives Publishing, Hampton Roads, Va.
ISBN 978-1-952773-80-8

ACKNOWLEDGMENTS

To my husband, Josh – who has been supportive of my writing from the beginning. He helped me pick up the pieces after the relationship described in this submission. I shudder to think how lost I would have been without him.

To my daughter, Liliana – may she never go through what I did. She is my source of strength as I finally put most of these writings together.

To Brieanna "Ducky" – a supportive friend who did her best to help me during the roughest times of the relationship. She's always given me honest advice and support.

To Angela – the unexpected friend I gained along the way. I'm so proud that we got out.

To Alan and Michelle – my first reviewers when I write something new. They've always given me encouragement and pushed me to continue.

To anyone that relates to the experiences in this book – I am so proud of you. Whether you have left the relationship or haven't found a way out yet, you are so strong. I believe in you. It does get better, and you do deserve happiness and safety.

And finally, to my publisher Teech! – who believed in my message before even reading the first poem.

CONTENTS

FIRST MEETING

13-year-old Girl
Meets 15-year-old Boy
Overachiever girl tries to get ahead
     Summer school for gym
Meets underachieving boy
     How do you fail gym class?
He's interested
I'm shy
We get along so beautifully
He's sweet and caring
I'm intelligent with a temper
Nothing happens this summer

But we hang out again later
Though I'm at a different school,
We talk on the phone often

Until I'm at his school
And we meet him again
He seems a little different
Maybe more grown up
But still sweet
We decide to date

This seals our fate

K

It's a new school
I know no one but him
Introduced to his friends
They seem nice and accepting
Except 1: K
K was **possessive**
He said it was "nothing"
He knew she liked him
But it was "nothing"
Continued to see each other

Until the day he called
I have a confession to make
Cheating
In her jacuzzi?

I should leave
But I don't
Benefit of the doubt
Maybe it won't happen again
I'm sure it does
Because K stays **possessive**

THE FIRST

Six months fly
We're getting closer all the time
We snuggle and he's so sweet
I'm finally feeling ready
16 years old
It's time

I give myself over to desire
I want him to be my first
      My only
           My forever

It stings so bad I cry
         How is this supposed to be enjoyable?
At least I love him
I'm dedicated
Maybe next time will be better

PROPOSAL

A few more weeks pass
We keep trying until we get it right
Until one night after
During the week of Christmas
We're cuddling, and he asks me
> *When you turn 18,*
> *Will you marry me?*
Of course!
I'm young
In love
I agree
He brings out jewelry
A necklace of small stones,
Baby sapphires and diamonds
Shaped like a circle, but not a "ring"
We're engaged

BITES

He wants to claim me
Not with a hickey
Like normal teens
But a bite
One strong enough to bruise
This idea excites me
Claiming? Owning?

Yes

I'm not prepared for it
The bite hurts
It's not just a bruise
But bloody
It's not easy to hide
My forearm looks like a target
For weeks

And the worst part about it
He wouldn't let me claim him back

PREDATOR AND PREY

Roleplay

He says we'll just pretend
I don't understand what we need to spice up
But that's what he suggests
I agree, it might be fun

Predator and prey

He chases me around the house
When he finally grabs me
He throws me on his bed
I'm laughing at first
As he pushes himself inside
No preparation or waiting
He thinks the game has been enough
Until I start to cry
To his credit, he does stop
He apologizes
Bangs his head against the wall
     and the door for hurting me
It seems like he feels bad
            I apologize to him
He didn't know how I was feeling
He thought it was a part of the game

This is the only time he apologizes like this for hurting me.

ANOTHER FIRST

I don't remember
The first time
He hits me
It was probably over something
Miniscule
Not important
During the heat of an argument
Perhaps
He apologizes
It will never happen again
It's a lie, of course

They always do it again

ISOLATION

It started gradually
One person at a time
> *I don't want you talking to them*

He would tell me how
They were untrustworthy,
They would hurt me
He was the only one
I could trust
I would tell them what he said
And some tried to fight
For me and our friendship
Most did not
And so it started
Until I was
> **Alone**

Except his friends,
The people he trusted
Who would not stop
What he was doing to me
> They were **afraid** of him

Like I was
They could not control him
Stop him
> For **fear** of him
>> Hurting me even more

AIRWAY

We experiment with
    Choking
During sex
    You'll love it
        He says
I learn to
    When he's doing it properly
    Leaving my airway clear
    Squeeze the sides
    That's the pleasurable way
But when he's angry
    And I'm left with no air
    I'm **terrified**
He says
    It'll never happen again
I believe him
    Until the next apology

SUMMER SCHOOL

He graduated before me
I wanted to be with him
So, I took the option
Double summer school
12 hours a day
5 days a week
All summer
He wasn't happy
We couldn't see each other
I thought one summer would be worth it
He didn't agree
So once again
He cheated

But this time
He didn't confess

THE CALL

The summer is about to end
When my phone rings
It's a girl named KK
And she has something very important to say
He cheated with me
She apologizes
No idea he had a girlfriend
Until a friend told her who knew
She said she never had been with someone
So fast
He seemed so nice
I heard she moved away
To Florida, I think
I hope she's happy now

I7TH BIRTHDAY

It was a long summer
But I did it!
High school graduation
College starts in 3 days
And I'm turning 17
I feel accomplished
But he's upset

You're getting ahead of me

He starts to complain
And mom won't let him around anymore
Now that she knows
About the first

I'm surprised
But she lets me spend the night out
A friend's house
The mom agrees she won't let him over
And my mom says okay
My first sleepover since I was a child
And I'm almost an adult

He throws a fit
Upset that he can't spend the night with me
It is my birthday, after all
And then he does something

So stupid
Controlling
Though I don't see it then

He tries to kill himself
Pills
On the phone with me
As he takes how many
Of whatever pill
Slurry words and then silence

I call the police
My first big panic attack
He's fine
Can sleep it off
But my birthday was ruined

COLLEGE

I don't notice the control
Until college is in full swing
We fight every week
Mostly about my new friends
We break up,
Get back together
            You're getting too far ahead of me
He continues to say that
He doesn't trust them
It feels like he doesn't trust me either
The sporadic violence is not so
Sporadic anymore
It's not serious, I think
It was good before
It can be good again
He convinces me to drop out
Leave my new freedom
And be with him
            alone

TWO GUYS

Before I leave college
Two guys
On separate nights
   Acquaintance rape
Both helped with rides to and from class
I was stuck
Instead of supporting me
   He used it as an excuse to claim
   I cheated
Now he's free to do what he wants
With whoever he wants
And I can't say anything

SPARK A FIRE

Desire and hatred
Mingle like friends
I want you more
When you reject me
The pain makes me return
Like a moth to the flame
I hate the pain
But I'm also sustained by it
I love you
I hate you
I need you
Fire burns me
Beneath my skin
Desire inflames it
And the hatred too
Ultimately,
Does it even matter
Who controls the fan?

NEGATIVE ENCOURAGEMENT

Struggle with self-harm
I have since I was 11
Ritualistic process
Biweekly at first
Until maybe once a year

We get together
Regression
Instead of wanting me well
He gives me encouragement
Of the wrong kind
                    You should hurt yourself
He tells me when we fight
                    Do it more
He says when I start to crack
                    Pain feels good

OUT OF REACH

One consequence
Of loving you is knowing
That my goals will never be achieved
You hated

               When I started to get ahead

Began my higher education
Met other people
How else could I finally
Get away from you,
If I could not see
The pathway out?
Holding me back
Was one way to
Keep me in a cage
This was not one
Of gilded gold, but
Cold, unyielding iron
Wrought from a gate
To hold me in

AT THE DUGOUT

It's winter
I'm 17 now
Dropped out of college
Not yet working
He wants sex so often
And doesn't allow for protection
Eventually
He thinks I'm pregnant
But doesn't say anything
We go to the dugout
At a nearby elementary school
He says *we should spar*
But this isn't normal
Repetitive punches to the abdomen
Tense up when I hit you
I'm in tears
It goes on
Feels like hours have passed
Before he stops
He was right
I didn't know
Not until the miscarriage
My baby
Gone because of their father
We couldn't have afforded it anyway

WELL-EARNED PUNISHMENT

I deserved it.

>I cheated in previous relationships.

I deserved it.

>I could never learn to listen.

I deserved it.

>We weren't ready for a baby.

I deserved it.

AT THE MALL

We go to the mall often
He spends my money
On things for him
I'm not allowed to complain
Because he's with me
       Head down
I can't meet people in the eye
Not worthy of doing it
Anymore
Especially to him
So, I stare at the floor
While he talks with people
If I displease him
He'll hit me
Even in public now
Doesn't matter who sees
       They know you deserve it
I know I do too
He doesn't accept back talk
My fiery temper has been reeled in
Smothered
By the fear of pain
I don't know what triggers him
But this trip
Instead of a hit
He kicks me
Between the legs

I manage to stay upright
Breathing through the pain
He does it again

Bruised pelvis bone

He laughs
　　　You should have fallen the first time
I agree
It would have been easier

CRUSHED UNDERFOOT

My heart does not belong
at your feet to be trampled

Yet here I am,

getting your boots ready
to squash this sinew
like grapes for wine

Brandi Dise

THE OTHER WOMAN

He's been cheating for a while
    Another girlfriend
    In a different city
He tells me about her
She's perfect in every way
    She knows how to listen to him
    She gives him what he wants
    I need to be more like her
He wants us to meet
    To be friends
We go halfway to a different mall
I'm not allowed to say anything
She can't know about me
    We're exes, just friends
      He says when he introduces her and I
She's hesitant but goes with it
I have no choice but to do the same
It's fun with the three of us
    But I need to tell her the truth
I try when we get have a moment alone
    She doesn't believe me
Knew I would say something
    Convince her to leave because
    I still love him
That much is true
    But I just don't want her hurt
    Like he's hurt me

Under My Skin:

I CHEATED

I have a breakdown
He tells me about who he's cheating with
He controls me
What I do, say, wear
I can't leave
He won't allow me
I'm his, remember?
But I need to break free somehow

There's an older neighbor
Our moms are friends
My mom would gladly have me date him instead

She doesn't say anything
When he's there all night
Even there the next morning
We begin an affair

He's freshly single
And I'm so alone
It goes on for months
I feel guilty for enjoying it

Soft touches
Friendship
I missed this
Feelings

I confess to him
But he stops the affair
I didn't start this to break up a relationship
I cry
Lonely again

PREGNANT AGAIN

The affair had ended
Several months before
When I found out
I'm pregnant
Too early to be anyone else's
I tell him
He's not excited
Not like me
I've been dreaming of babies
Since I lost the last
       Fat
       He calls me
When I've barely gained a pound
My mom isn't thrilled
She tells me she will
       Babysit using Velcro on their hair
       to the ceiling
I cry for **my baby**
To be born with only one person
Who really wants them
Everyone calls for an abortion
I shouldn't have given in —
given up **my baby**
I make it to 11 weeks before I crack
I regret it the rest of my life

MOVE OUT

The aftermath of the
Abortion
Makes me have to move out
From my mom's
To a friend's house
She's still in high school
Senior year
I go back to college again
Work part-time to cover rent
Now he and I can really be together
I was happy
Excited
I thought things could finally go back
To what they were 3 years ago
But I'm wrong
He's even more controlling now
He comes over when he wants
And I have to be waiting for him
Alone
He buys my clothes
I don't have choices
He doesn't like that I'm in school again
But my friend's mom insisted
Or I wouldn't have a place to live

The physical violence before
Is nothing compared to now
My friend knows what he's doing
She's upset but feels powerless
I insist I love him
You're an idiot
She tells me, as I cry

ACQUIRED TASTE

Your silver tongue
Is so sweet in my mouth
I can taste you
Through the acridness
Of the alcohol
The cigarettes and marijuana
I reach back
To the flavor of you
Before the bitterness
Took root
The realization hits
That I'm looking for an ideal
Something I once loved
But was never meant to stay
It hits hard
When I'm finally alone
The memories of your flavor
On the tip of my tongue

YOU CAN'T FIX HIM

You can't fix him
But he can break you
Down into little pieces
For someone else
To rebuild

You can't fix him
He doesn't want the help
He thinks he's fine
Even though all he does
Is hurt women

He doesn't need the help
He's perfect as he is
Emotionally and physically
Unbroken and smooth
You can't fix him

He tried to break you
Grind you into dust
Beyond the point of help
Or being put back together
You can't fix him

THE WALL

My new house saw so much
    Violence

Every argument turned physical
And we fought often
Usually about his cheating
He wasn't hiding anything now
I was seeing his full self

    And I loved and hated him

This time, he grabbed my throat
Nothing new
But he threw me into the wall too
That was a first
He accused me of cheating
    So, what if I was?

I couldn't leave or I would have

My head and back hit the wall
I saw spots
    Concussion
Don't understand how there wasn't
    A me-sized dent

EXPRESSIONS OF PAIN

Fake smiles
Used to cover up
The truth, the pain
A facade
Meant to shield

Myself, and everyone else

It takes so much energy
To keep it posted
At my gate
I'm struggling to
Survive
But you are
Thriving
Off my anguish

POST-ARGUMENT APPEARANCES

We are reflections of each other
Your eyes are dull, unfeeling
You don't want the argument
Hate the accusations I give
Because they are true
> *You just want me to behave*
> *Like a good girl*
> *In the box you created*

While emotions fill my eyes
The tears that come
When my rage hits the
> *Stratosphere*
Until the tables turn
And I'm broken instead
Crumpled in a heap
> As my anger fueled
> Your fists

END OF DAYS

I thought I was going to die.
This night, here with you.
Your hands around my throat.
My sight going black around the edges.
I thought I was going to die.
I struggle against you.
You are too strong for me.
I may just give up.
I thought I was going to die.
You have brainwashed me.
I think this is love. How romantic it is,
to die by the hand of your lover.

And yet, I live.
You let go of my throat.
Stinging rush of air to my lungs.
Vision comes back.
And yet, I live.
Your hands change to hit instead.
Bruises are already forming.
I beg you to stop.
And yet, I live.
You leave me in a heap.
I cry in pain and alone.
But I am alive another day.

MISSED VISITATION

The hour is late
   The clocks says 1
You were supposed to be here
   Hours ago
And yet, I can feel you
   Miles away

I know in my soul
That you are
  With another woman
While I lie here
Tossing and turning
   Alone

SUICIDAL/MURDEROUS TENDENCIES

Is a death that you desire
At the hands of your lover
Suicide or Murder?
That's the question I ask myself
As I lose the ability to breathe
Once more
My life is literally in your hands
Morbid thoughts of romanticism
I truly want to die
Here in your hands

BED OF NAILS

I've crumpled
Become but a pile
of flesh
Zigzagging scars
Underneath the surface
and bruised on top
I feel you
On me
Inside of me
Joining with me
To get your own rocks off
My pleasure matters no more
Just a vessel for you
Laying in this bed
I made by staying
But leaving
Would hurt worse

UNDER MY SKIN

You can see the bruises
In my daze
I find them beautiful
If hauntingly so
Romantic
Gifts from my lover
There are others
Invisible
Deeper layers of tissue hurt
So tender to the touch
My psyche is also bruised

HELLO, DARKNESS

Flying high
The sensation as my brain
is slowly
Starved
of necessary oxygen
Hands around my throat
Bring me higher still
Summons darkness
Consciousness slipping
You release me
Finally
Sharp inhale of breath
I'm alive
I love the thrill
Pushing the edge
I'm scared though
For this was not
My request
Done in anger
Not safe, sane, or
Consensual

THIRD TIME IS THE CHARM

It isn't long before I find out
I'm pregnant again
No one can talk me out of it
I'm so excited
Again, he is not
I don't have the pressure from my family
I keep this baby
Past the abortion deadline
She lives through the violence
Through the sickness
The stress of everything
My friend wants to help
So does her mom
We buy little baby clothes
In pastel pinks, greens, yellows
My baby
I want the best for her I can give
Her father is not the best
But I think he can try

BREAKING DOWN

Cracks

They form slowly
Gradually,

Over time
Small pains at first

Until it chisels away
At my psyche, heart, body
I feel you

Getting in the crevices

Becoming a part of me
That's hard to break away from
I hate the pain

Or do I?

I keep coming back for it
Masochistically
Until there's nothing left
Of me to dissolve

THREATS

If you don't, I'll-
    You'll what?
    Hit me?
    Like you haven't done that before.

You know what will happen if you-
    Yeah, I do know.
    Pain.
    Physical, mental, and emotional.

Why can't you be more like-
    Oh, your other girlfriends?
    The one who is "more perfect in every way?"
    Who listens to everything you say?

Got it.
    You put me through so much abuse.
    Tormented me for years.
    Do you like the same threats?

Brandi Dise

EARTHWORM

You wormed your way
  Inside me
  Squiggling through the layers
  Of dirt and pain
  To join with me

An impostor
  In my body
  Beneath my bones
  In the very sinew

Made your way
  Into my heart
  And brain
  To lay the eggs
  Of my future destruction

No Excuse

You made me-
> He claims, as the bruises already start to form,
> marks flourishing from the site where
> the impact occurred only minutes before

If you only hadn't-
> He says, like it changes what he did,
> whether through kicks, bites, smacks, or punches

You should have dropped it-
> He declares, after he grabs me by the throat
> hard and long enough for my vision to blacken
> and I fall to the ground

You need to learn to listen-
> He remarks, even though I try my best to avoid his anger
> for fear of his wrathful retribution through force

It's for your own good-
> He whispers, trying to console my crying
> with his ineffectual excuses and lies, confusing me
> with sudden kindness when before
> there had been only pain

LACK OF AUTONOMY

Your demands
Have robbed me of everything
My choices, gone
It is up to you how I
Wear my hair
Style my clothes
Speak to people
Exist in a world
Where I'm nothing
but your plaything
Set in the example
Of your ideals
You want me and the others
To be exactly alike
Replicas of your dream
Instead of the individuals
You stripped
Of their freedom of choice

LIES AT HOME

Fake smile
Not a hair out of place
New clothes
Posh and polished
No one suspects or knows
My own personal truth
How we live daily
How I survive at home
      With a *Monster*
The mental abuse started first
Small things, insignificant
He must have just had a bad day
      He didn't mean to say that
But then it was physical
      Not too hard, only an   'accident'
Empty apologies
      "It will never happen again"
Until it did, and it was worse
Bruises, hidden under clothes
      And makeup
Blood, wiped away with cloth
      Stained by the *Monster*
Choking, no air
Thrown against the wall
Bruised back and shoulders

Now I can't wear my bikini
    Or everyone will know
Sex was not always fun
    Forced instead
        But he said it "wasn't him"
Another personality who didn't like
    'Something I did'
    "You deserved what you got"
Leave me alone!
Don't touch me!
    "You like it!"
No!
    You're a *Monster*!
I know the truth
    Even if no one else does

TRUTH IS COMING

Lies
I've gotten so tired of them

My lies
And Yours
Our love is fading
Broken promises
Again and again
Cracking facade
Fooling no one
I know about the others

You think you know mine
The truth obscured
By years of layered
Lies

SERRATED

I'm covered in
Jagged edges,
     left over from the broken promises
        of people who
           "loved" me

Who said they would never leave

Afraid of my own skin,
     the shadows within
     the scars in my veins,
     in my bones

I'm not yet ready
To peel back the layers
     to show the real me
     underneath the surface
How could anyone
     want me
        under this damaged skin?

LEAVING

I found out he's cheating again
After he promised to stop
That's it
I'm finally finished
> *Let me see you*
> *one more time*
He wants to talk it out
Like we always have in the past
I agree to his terms
Not at my house, but up the street
Late at night, alone
Hours of going back and forth
In his anger, he throws my phone
It shatters on the asphalt
I can see he's not going to change
And I tell him so
> *If I can't have you,*
> *you can't have the baby*
He punches me in the stomach
28 weeks pregnant
I see it coming
As I have so often before
And I manage to step back
Avoid the worst of the blow
It still connects
My new maternal instincts kick in
> *Must protect my baby*
If I was going back, I refuse now
Nothing will change my mind

TURN A BLIND EYE

Eyes
They say
Are the windows to the soul
To the pain
And suffering
The joy
And happiness

Eyes also show
The emptiness
A vacancy created by trauma
The thousand yard stare
Is a fitting title
When eyes see nothing
And the person
Feels everything

PLAN WENT AWRY

I don't know what the plan was
When 15-year-old me
Decided to have a boyfriend
But it wasn't this
The pain and scars stay
Longer than the relationship did
I didn't make it out
Unharmed
But I am thankful
To be free

FIGHT OR FLIGHT

Will the day finally come
When I can hear your name
And my heart doesn't stop
My throat get dry, sticky
From fear
That the pain will come back
When I say the wrong thing
My stomach twists
With anxiety
Heart feels constricted
I need to
Prepare to run away
Hide to stay safe
Will that day ever come?
I hope so
Maybe soon

D

Almost 4 Years
4 years too long
Too violent
Too terrible
I don't want to remember,
But I do
I think about it sometimes
Though not as much as I used to
I do not miss you,
Not one little bit
Not your "love", nor your hate
Or the feeling of being hit
Abuse and terror were common
For us, just how things were
Whereas you used to control my emotions,
They finally no longer stir.

REFORGING BONDS

A few years pass
Until I break free
Using my own strength
I begin to reach out
To those I pushed away
I apologize
Those who do answer
Respond in kind
They could see
What was happening
Even when I was still wearing
Rose-colored glasses
I make back a few friends
But many never come back

PLAYING WITH MUD

Many times over the course
Of our relationship,
I felt stuck
In time, place
Torn between
A rock and a hard place
Saying something
      Reacting
           Fighting back
Just to be smothered
      Beaten
           Tied down
It didn't matter
If it was with you
Or with my mom
I was so
Stuck
And now I still feel
Frozen
Trapped in the past
Where my memories
Drown me in mud
Fill my lungs with your
Thick, toxic sludge
Without a hope of fresh air

I DON'T WANT TO
SHED A TEAR

I don't want to shed a tear,
> but you make me, with the way I am treated.

I don't want to shed a tear,
> but I don't know what else to do when I'm stuck
> between rock and a hard place.

I don't want to shed a tear,
> but it's all I can for as I sit here in the darkness,
> waiting for you to return.

I don't want to shed a tear,
> but all I see in my mind's eye is the two of you
> together.

I don't want to shed a tear,
> but I keep thinking about the broken promises
> you made about not being like everyone else.

I don't want to shed a tear,
> but I keep thinking about the choice
> I'm going to have to make.

I don't want to shed a tear,
> but I keep wondering why things like this
> always happen to me.

I don't want to shed a tear,
> but I remember that even the ring you gave me
> was a lie.

I don't want to shed a tear,
> but I'm recalling all of the happy times years past.

Under My Skin:

I don't want to shed a tear,
  but I'm wishing those happy times will come back.
I don't want to shed a tear,
  but I hear you walk through the door finally
  at 3 in the morning, smelling like alcohol and sex.
I don't want to shed a tear,
  as you call me names and tell me again
  how she's so much better than me in every way.
I don't want to shed a tear,
  as I scream, I'm done, and start to pack.
I don't want to shed a tear,
  when I come back and
  you're threatening me not to leave.
I don't want to shed a tear,
  as you pick me up by my throat and throw me
  across the room.
I don't want to shed a tear,
  when you threaten me again as I go to leave
  for good.
I don't want to shed a tear,
  as I close the door behind me and breathe
  the fresh air of freedom for the first time in four years.

UNDESIRED REFLECTIONS
ON THE PAST

Often lately
      memories
Have been coming to the surface. I have been trying hard to forget these
      memories.
Instead, these
      memories
Have been bubbling to the surface. Though
      memories
Are individual to the person and the time, these
      memories
Need to stay in the past.

I do not want to
      remember
The abuse you made me endure. I do not want to
      remember
The pain that you made me feel. I do not want to
      remember
The nights that I spent crying, alone. I do not want to
      remember
The few good times there were. I do not want to
      remember
the four years we spent together.

It is difficult to
      forget
The times you showed me love. It is difficult to
      forget
The feeling of helplessness and defeat. It is difficult to
      forget
The feeling of your body against mine. It is difficult to
      forget
The sting of your hand across my face and body. It is difficult to
      forget
That I did truly love you.

SPOKEN TO THE PAST

If I could tell you anything
It would be thank you
For showing me how
I'm *not* supposed to be treated
How *not* to be spoken to
That I **am** important
I **do** matter
I **am** enough
Without knowing how bad
You were
I might have never known
How good he is

NEGATIVE SENSATIONS

Even now
10 years later
There are days when
I can still feel you
Smell your cologne
Your voice in my ear
The sensations are so real

I'm overwhelmed
Struggling

Wanting a cigarette and
a stiff drink
Trying to smother down
The memories and sensations
You left me with

MOVING ON

I know what you've done,
     As well as you do.
But I can no longer run
     And neither can you.
I will live my life,
     Separate as I must do.
I am now a wife;
     My family will never know you.
They know what you've done,
     As well as I do.
Now I can be *someone*,
     Though the same cannot be said of you.
I have ridden my life of your taint,
     As I knew I must do.
I keep my feelings under restraint,
     But I will never again care for you.
I am finally moving on.

10 YEARS SINCE

The punch that ended it all
The final straw

> *If I can't have you*
> *You can't have the baby*

The last insults
Hurled in my face
A broken phone
Thrown on the concrete in anger

And yet
I still noted your birthday
Earlier this week
I still feel your hands
Around my throat
Hear your voice
In my ears
Experience the fear
In my heart

And yet
Something still doesn't feel real

> *It wasn't that bad, was it?*

I can't remember bruises
I never documented anything

> *Was it as bad as I remember?*

UPDATES

Sometimes friends message me
Say how you are
What you're doing
Who you're with
I don't ask for it
They come to me
That's how I know
About the first arrest
(child support)
The eviction
T leaving
(the same reasons I did)
The move to Florida
M leaving
(yep, same thing!)
But she called the police
So there's also
A second arrest
And probation
For domestic violence
I'm relieved that these women
Can leave
But I worry
That someone will eventually
End up dead
At your hands

GROWTH AND DEVELOPMENT

Struggling with myself
Over how worthy I am
Of love, kindness,
Basic human decency
Has led me down a path
Where I've disregarded
My own needs
Emotional and physical alike
I haven't loved myself
Enough to take care of me
Or make anyone else
Respect me
In the wake of my new
Physical conditions
Resulting from trauma, stress,
My own perception of
Unworthiness,
I must stand firm
For what's right
For me, my body, my family
If I have to fight
My illnesses
With medication, I will
I've already eliminated
Those who don't help me grow
Now I need to put the work in
To blossom

HINDSIGHT

Looking back
I don't understand
How I stayed
As long as I did
With the turmoil
You put me through
Almost 4 years
Of anguish
A short honeymoon period
Before the tough times started
The lies were first
Then rough words
Meant to tear me down
Did their job
Making it easier
For you to turn physical
After all
No one wants me anyway
No eye contact
Head down in public
Hits, kicks, bites
Bruises under clothes
Some stay for a month
                But I love him!
I proclaim
Friends try to help
They see what happens

But they are scared of him too
One, two, three pregnancies
You cause the first loss
The second is on me
But the last
You almost made me lose too
Punching a 7 month pregnant woman
In the stomach
Is **deplorable**
Even for you
The final straw
I can't stay anymore
I was planning to leave anyway
But now is the time
I haven't turned back
Even as you approach me
Several times
Over various social media
You refuse to be there
For the daughter
You helped to create
The son
You forced on another
The kids are better off
Like their mothers
Without you
Your violence
Abuse
And lies

BIOGRAPHY

Brandi Dise is a poet living in Virginia Beach, Virginia. She was recently featured by *Silent Spark Press* in the e-book and physical book *Remarkable Poetry* (Volume 8 for the physical copy). She was also featured in the Fall/Winter 2022 edition of the online literature magazine *Wicked Gay Ways*. Two of her poems will be featured in the first volume of the e-magazine *7 Deadly Thoughts*.

The first in her immediate family to graduate from college, she received her bachelor's degree from Old Dominion University in 2020. When she is not writing, Brandi enjoys spending time with her family & pets, reading fiction, and watching anime.

colophon

Brought to you by Wider Perspectives Publishing, care of James Wilson, with the mission of advancing the poetry and creative community of Hampton Roads, Virginia.
This page used to have many cute and poetic expressions, but the sheer number of quality artists deserving mention has superseded the need to art. This has become some serious business; please check out how *They art...*

Faith May Griffin
Tabetha Moon House
Travis Hailes- Virgo, thePoet
Nick Marickovich
Grey Hues
Rivers Raye
Madeline Garcia
Chichi Iwuorie
Symay Rhodes
Tanya Cunningham-Jones
    (Scientific Eve)
Terra Leigh
Raymond M. Simmons
Samantha Borders-Shoemaker
Taz Weysweete'
Jade Leonard
Darean Polk
Bobby K.
    (The Poor Man's Poet)
J. Scott Wilson (TEECH!)
Gloria Darlene Mann
Neil Spirtas
Jorge Mendez & JT Williams
Sarah Eileen Williams
Shanya – Lady S.

Jason Brown (Drk Mtr)
Ken Sutton
Kailyn Rae Sasso
Crickyt J. Expression
Se'Mon-Michelle Rosser
Lisa M. Kendrick
Cassandra IsFree
Nich (Nicholis Williams)
Samantha Geovjian Clarke
Natalie Morison-Uzzle
Gus Woodward II
Patsy Bickerstaff
Arlandria Speaks
Jack Cassada
Dezz
Catherine TL Hodges
Linda Spence-Howard
Martina Champion
... and others to come soon.

the Hampton Roads
    Artistic Collective
    (757 Perspectives) &
The Poet's Domain
are all WPP literary journals in cooperation with Scientific Eve or Live Wire Press

Check for those artists on FaceBook, Instagram, the Virginia Poetry Online channel on YouTube, and other social media.

Hampton Roads Artistic Collective is an extension of WPP which strives to simultaneously support worthy causes in Hampton Roads and the local creative artists.

Made in the USA
Middletown, DE
16 July 2024